Original
B.B. King

An annotated guide
to the guitar
technique of B.B. King

by Jesse Gress

Amsco Publications
New York/London/Sydney/Cologne

Exclusive Distributors:

Music Sales Corporation
225 Park Avenue South, New York, NY 10003 USA

Music Sales Limited
8/9 Frith Street, London W1V 5TZ England

Music Sales Pty. Limited
120 Rothschild Street, Rosebery, Sydney,
NSW 2018, Australia

US ISBN 0.8256.2540.8
UK ISBN 0.7119.0961.X
Order No. AM 63504

Arranged and compiled by Jesse Gress
Music edited by Peter Pickow
Text edited by Amy Appleby
Book layout and design by Leonard Vogler
Cover photographs by L.F.I.
Interior photographs by Luciano Viti/Retna Ltd.,
Darryl Pitt/Retna, Ltd., Nourry/Stills,
David Redfern/Retna, Ltd., Andrea Laubach/
Retna, Ltd., Larry Busaca/Retna, Ltd., Gary
Gershoff/Retna, Ltd.

Printed in the United States Of America by
Vicks Lithograph and Printing Corporation

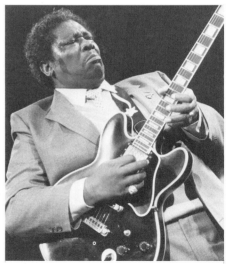

To Charylu, with love.

Acknowledgments

Thanks to the following people for making this book possible: Peter Pickow, Kathy Lombard, Barrie Edwards, Charylu Roberts, Wolf Marshall, Tom Wheeler, Steve Kimock, Eric Schenk, my parents (Doc and Ginnie), all of my teachers and students, and, of course, to the great B.B. King.

Special thanks to Danny Caron for transcriptions of "You Upsets Me, Baby," "Every Day I Have the Blues," and "Woke Up This Morning," and for sharing his stylistic insights (and letting me borrow his 335!).

Introduction

B.B. King is not only the king of the blues, he is a model among men. His philosophy of life and dedication to his art form the cornerstone of a remarkable career dedicated to self-improvement and universal brotherhood. As an entertainer, he has touched people of all ages, races, and creeds. As a musician, his influence has no boundaries. In the 1960s, his guitar playing was adopted as "the truth" by a younger generation of guitarists, including Michael Bloomfield, Eric Clapton, and Jimi Hendrix. As each successive generation of guitarists continues to build on the ideas of the last, it becomes apparent that B.B. King is responsible for much of today's rock and blues guitar vocabulary. His playing features many elusive techniques interpreted from his own life experiences and his innate "feel" for music.

Blues music is a tradition passed on orally and through recordings. To play the blues, one must feel and hear them. To hear the blues, there is no better place to start than with the music of B.B. King. To say that his recording career has been prolific is an understatement. B.B. has recorded over seventy albums and one hundred singles in the last forty years—and every one is a winner. As a role model, he offers much to any ambitious person. T*he Arrival of B.B. King*, by Charles Sawyer, is an inspiring biography of the artist which details his distinguished career and accomplishments.

In *Original B.B. King*, the artist's guitar style is examined by extracting lines from some of his classic solos and analyzing them individually. Most masters of improvisation think in terms of short, pre-learned phrases. Their true art comes to light in the way that they spontaneously reorganize these ideas into longer lines. This book is designed to help you isolate and understand these valuable phrases, so that they can become ingrained in your musical memory. As a result, you will be able to summon them at will in a wide variety of musical situations. Also included are complete choruses from some of B.B.'s most famous solos.

B.B. King is a master of musical form and development. He can build a solo from slow simmer to a rapid boil in two or three choruses, increasing tension and adding new themes with each chorus. His live recordings and all-too-infrequent instrumental albums provide the best examples of these solos, and are well worth checking out. Rounding out this book are ideas for expanding B.B. King's lines into new and interesting blues patterns. There's also a helpful listing of B.B. King–style chord voicings and progressions, and a comprehensive discography.

So, if you're just getting into the blues, grab your guitar, some B.B. King albums, this book, and go for it. If you've already been playing the blues for a while, this book will provide many new insights to sharpen your musical ability. When B.B. King was first honing his talents, there was no "King of the Blues" to learn from. Although he drew inspiration and technical skills from Blind Lemon Jefferson, Charlie Christian, Django Reinhardt, Bukka White, T-Bone Walker, and others, he had to invent his own techniques to bring life to the sounds stirring in his imagination. I hope that this book will help you to do the same.

And now, to echo the introduction that has been heard on as many as three hundred stages a year for the past four decades, "Ladies and gentlemen, the King of the Blues, Mr. B.B. King!"

An Interview with B.B. King

by Tom Wheeler

When were you born, and where did you grow up?

I was born in 1925 in the country outside of Itta Bena, Mississippi, which is not too awful far from Indianola. My parents separated when I was around four, and I spent some time in the hills of Mississippi, up around Kilmichael. That's where I lost my mother, when I was nine. I was a farmhand all of my life, until I was inducted into the Army and sent to Camp Shelby near Hattiesburg, Mississippi, in 1943. I was plowing, driving tractors and trucks, chopping cotton—everything that one does on a farm. I did some of it.

When did you first encounter music?

The first music was in church. From that time until now, that... certain something was instilled into me. I had been baptized as a Baptist, then I was in the Holiness—the Church of God in Christ—and the singing and the music in the churches was something that a small boy, even in his fifties today, will never forget.

What did your family think of you playing the blues when you started?

I couldn't play them at home. I was formerly a spiritual singer, and they wouldn't go for the blues, not around the house *[laughs, shakes his head]* not then. That's one thing about the early days of the blues. A few of the spiritual people *liked* the blues, but they would play *their* blues after twelve, when they were in their room and nobody could hear them. But you always had a few devils like myself and a few others that would listen to *anything.* You played it and it sounded good, we would listen to it. I was singing spirituals in my first group, the Elkhorn Singers, but I'd love to go to juke joints at that time.

When did you begin playing professionally?

In the middle 1940s, in Indianola, on the corner of Church and Second Street. Second Street is like the main part of town, and Church Street crossed it and went into the black area, what we called "across the tracks." I never passed the hat, but the people knew that I'd appreciate a dime if I played a tune they'd requested.

Do you remember your first paying job as a musician?

I don't remember my first paid gig, but I remember the first gig where I started working for like a week at a time—1949 that was, in West Memphis, at a place called the 16th Street Grill. That lady was paying me $12.00 a night, room and board. I was 24 years old, and that was more money—I didn't know there was that much money in the world. So that's how that started. That was me alone up there—sing, and then play, as I normally do. Sing and play. Working there made me think about going on the radio as a disc jockey, because the lady at the grill told me that if I could get my own show like [harmonica player] Sonny Boy Williamson and [blues guitarist] Bobby Nighthawk and quite a few of the guys, she would give me a steady weekly job, and I *loved* that idea.

How did you acquire the name "B.B."?

The idea came from the local radio station where I was working, WDIA. I was singing some advertisements for Pepticon, one of these cure-all patent medicines. Later, when I became a disc jockey, with my own one-hour show, they would call me "the blues boy," or "the boy from Beale Street." A lot of times they'd shorten it to B.B., and I liked that, and it stuck with me all this time.
Before you were nationally recognized, was there much contact between you and your contemporaries such as Muddy Waters? Were you aware of each other; did you have each other's records and so forth?

No, I had *their* records, but see, Muddy Waters and John Lee Hooker and all of those guys were playing *before* me, and they didn't know me from Adam. I was *plowin'* when they was *playing'! [laughs]* I liked them, and I imagine that they were aware of each other. But they didn't know anything about me, no.

Compared to many electric guitarists, you play few notes.

I was at the Apollo Theater one time, and there was a critic there, and to me what he said was one of the great compliments that people have given me. The critic wrote: "B.B. King sings, and then Lucille sings." That made me feel very good, because I do feel that I'm still singing when I play. That's why I don't play a lot of notes maybe like some people. Maybe that's the reason why most of my music is very simple—that's the way I sing. When I'm playing a solo, I hear me singing through the guitar.

Did you play rhythm guitar first?

No. I never accompanied myself, still can't. I *cannot* play and sing at the same time; I just can't do it. I've always been featured from the very beginning. I still can't play rhythm worth anything, because I never had the chance to really play in a rhythm section. But I know a few chords.

Let's put it this way: I won't say I invented it, but they weren't doing it before I started. *[laughs]* I will say that I'm still trying. Bukka White and quite a few other people used bottlenecks. As I said, I got stupid fingers. They won't work. If I get something like that in my hand and try to use it, it just won't work. So my ears told me that when I trilled my hand, I'd get a sound similar to the sound they were getting with a bottleneck. And so for about thirty-two or thirty-three years I've been trying to do it, and now they tell me that I'm doing a little better.

What about the idea of hitting the fret a step lower than the intended note and bending it up—were people doing that before you?

Yes, but I'd never heard anybody do it the way I do it. My reason was that my ears don't always hear like they should. I'm always afraid that I might miss a note if I try to hit it right on the head, so if I hit down and slide up to it, my ears tell me when I get there. But also it's more like a violin or a voice; you just gliss up to it.

Your record collection is something of a legend.

Well, I've got over 30,000 records now. You won't believe this, but even though they're not alphabetized I can always tell if one's missing. One day I plan to get me one of these home computers and enter them all into that. Every time I go home I just tape, tape, tape.

Do you play visualized patterns on the fingerboard, or do you hear a note or phrase in your head before you hit it on the guitar?

I hear it first, sure do. It's like some guys use an electronic tuner and just look at the needle on the meter, but I can't buy that; I have to hear it, and it's the same with a phrase. No one else can set your hat on your head in a way that suits you. I don't think I've ever seen anybody that when you put their hat on their head they didn't take their hand and move it, even if it's just a bit. Well, I'm like that with the guitar. Do it your own way. When I play it's like trying to describe something to someone; it's a conversation where you say something in a certain way. A lot of times I play with my eyes closed, but in my mind I can still see the people paying attention to what I'm doing. I can see them as if they're saying, "Yeah, okay, I get it." Playing the guitar is like telling the truth—you never have to worry about repeating the same thing if you told the truth. You don't have to pretend, or cover up. If someone asks you again, you don't have to think about it or worry about it. To me, playing is the same way, if you put yourself into it, instead of something else, then when you get out there on the stage the next time, you don't have to worry, because there it is. It's you.

Today you're doing things on guitar that sound different from what you were doing only six months ago. Your style seems to continue to grow.

Well, I hope so, because I do study. People hold it against me sometimes. They say, "You're not playing the same thing that you played the last time." But I don't *want* to play the same thing I played last time. That would get boring. I always try to add something, or maybe take something away, to give it a little twist.

Does working with other instruments alter your approach to guitar?

Yes, it affects my phrasing, and it makes me a little more fluent. It's something for me to do when I'm not practicing like I should. I usually practice mentally, but when it comes to physical practice, I'm a little lazy. I don't know how it is with other musicians, but with me sometimes I don't play like I want to, and then I get a little bit disgusted and lay off for a while. Then one day, something happens, and I can't wait to get back to it.

You mentioned mental practice.

Sometimes I hear something—someone will walk by and whistle, or I'll hear it on the music in a restaurant—and I'll start to look at the fingerboard in my mind to see how I'd do it. I visualize the different ways to do it. That's a good thing to do; it helps you learn the guitar. Just don't do it too much when you're driving, or you'll forget where you're going. *[laughs]*

Do you read music?

Reading music is what I call spellin'. I *spell*, I read slowly. If the metronome is not goin' *too* fast, I can do it pretty good.

What brought about your recognition on an international scale?

That has to do with many things, like the changing of times, like the marching, and like the people getting together and trying to stamp out prejudice and all of the many, many things. It seemed to bring people together. It started out to make people think, to see that everybody had something to offer, and that if you listen carefully you could learn something from others. People started searching for the truth... while I've been diggin' all this time. Black awareness—there was a time if you called me black, it was insulting *[he nods]* oh yeah, insulting. In Mississippi we always did call white people white people but we, as a whole, really didn't want to be called black. We felt that at the time it was degrading, because it seemed that the person calling you black was really saying *more* than what they said. But later on we started to think about it. If the Indian is a red man, and the Chinese is a yellow man, and you're a white man, then why *not* be a black man? Everybody got aware, and became proud of the fact that we are what we are. We began to feel that we *did* have something to be proud of. Like when James Brown made "I'm Black and I'm Proud," this really hit a lot of us, and I think all of this has to do with the blues. There was a time when we felt that nobody else had dirty clothes in the closet, you know—the troubles of life. We were sort of made to feel like we were the only ones that had dirty clothes in the closet, and any time somebody said something to us or about us, we always felt that we should close the door and not let 'em know what we had in the closet.

And that finally began to change?

Yes. After the early sixties and all that, it's a funny thing, we come to find out that *everbody* has dirty clothes in the closet, and if the people in Nashville and Kentucky can be proud of bluegrass music—which is real music about the way they live, and about their problems, and their happiness and all—why *not* be proud of the blues? This kind of transition caused people to recognize the blues singers. Even the people who don't dig blues come up to me and say that they respect what I'm doing.

What do you look for in a musician who comes to work for you?

A man. I look for a man first, and a musician second. I must respect what he has to offer. I wouldn't say that a guy that can really blow the roof off a building is necessarily the best musician. He may be fiery; he's the type of guy that can really move an audience in a hurry. But an audience don't like to stand on its nose all the time. They want to get down and be something else from time to time. Then you've got another guy that has a touch when he's playing that he can really move people, like in a slow groove. Well, you don't want *that* all night. Each guy is good for his one particular thing. Everybody in my group is behind me to push me. I need their cooperation. But I look for someone who's 100% man. If he's only 50% musician, that's okay; we'll turn him into 75% musician after a while. But if he is not 100% man, there's nothing I can do.

B.B. King on Equipment and Technique

I don't have any calluses on my hands at all. This is because I keep the bridge set so the strings are close to the neck. That way, I don't have to press as hard as many people do on a larger gauge string.

My guitar is a Gibson ES 355. I like it because it has a long slender neck and the body balances very well. I don't use any settings, according to some people. Some guitarists, when they use the word setting, mean "Set to 1, to 5" etc. But I set my guitar according to how it sounds to me when I'm playing and I never look down to see what I'm doing. I just rotate the volume controls with my fingers, one finger moving forward or backwards against the two volume controls to make it wide open or close it.

However, I keep my amp wide open all the time. I do that so, when I need extra power, I get it from the guitar, instead of having to go to the amp and set it. The only exception is in a recording studio. Then, I record with my amp very low, never loud. But even when recording, I work my guitar settings as described above.

As most people know, my Gibson guitar is a stereo. I keep one channel closed on bass, and I leave treble wide open. I've got funny ears. Anything that's real bass, I can't hear very well to tell whether it's in tune or not. Because of that, I turn all the treble up on my instrument—so I can hear better.

As far as I'm concerned, the amplifier is not the most important thing. It's good as long as it amplifies the sound; that is, as long as it does what it's supposed to do. Other added features are OK and good for a lot of people, but for me, if it just amplifies, that's what I want. Of course, I turn a little bit of the echo on, which enhances my music, but I don't use much—just a little.

Bending Notes

When I bend notes I push up first; I never pull down. I see many younger guitarists who grab a string and pull down on it, but I never do. When bending notes, I use all my fingers, but the first three more than the little one.

Vibrato

I think that the best thing I've done is learning to trill in such a way that I create a sound similar to that produced by a person using a bottleneck. Trying to get that effect is what started me working on my vibrato. Also, I think I phrase a bit differently from most other guitarists. There's no real way to describe in words how I play the guitar. In order to really describe to someone how I get my sound, I'd have to show them.

I try my best to make my left hand trill evenly without any effort. For example, when I *try* to produce an even vibrato with my voice, it's very difficult, but when I just sing out naturally, the trill comes out even with no effort at all. Of course, a great deal of practice is necessary before the hand attains the dexterity required to move smoothly enough to get that vibrato. I want to make it just like my heart beat, something I don't have to think about at all. When I want to vary the speed of my vibrato, I try to create the same effect as when you get frightened and your heart speeds up, or when you relax and your heart slows down.

I don't trill like the average person on a violin. A violinist trills his hand from the front of the violin to the body, and most guitarists do the same thing. But my vibrato is not like that. Mine is kind of like a steady pulse, pushing the string up and pulling it down, or pushing it up and letting it go, without actually losing control of it. That's *wrong*—but it's the right way for me. All you have to do is push the string with an even flow, up and back, up and back, because if you keep practicing this, finally you can control it.

Right-Hand Picking Technique

I play mostly downstrokes, which is why I'm not very fast. I use a medium pick that isn't very flexible at all. I'm old-fashioned: I was taught to hold it with two fingers in the first place, so I still do it that way most times. I *hold* it with my thumb and index, and *control* it with my middle finger.

Now, I play pretty hard. I attack the strings harder than most people. A jazz player would never strike the strings as hard as I do, and neither would a lot of rockers. I fight the strings at times for presence, to get that force.

Soloing

Stay close to the melody. Play around the tonic note, pretty near the tonic chord. You can extend the progression a little, but do it with feelin'—bend it, pull it, tease it, get everything you can out of that one note. I never get too far out on a limb myself—unless I'm in my room where it doesn't matter so much. I know a half-step up or down is usually relative to where you're playing, but I don't like those distant sounds. I'm really a guy that loves to try a churchy type of sound.

Notation and Tablature

Vibrato.

Hammeron:
Pick a string and hold the note while striking a second, higher note with another finger. This causes the string to sound without being picked.

Pulloff:
Finger both notes. Pick the string, then pull off with the upper finger to sound the lower note.

Combined hammeron and pulloff

Half-step bend:
Pick the string and bend the note up one half-step.

Whole-step bend:
Pick the string and bend the note up one whole step.

Minor third bend:
Pick the string and bend the note up one and one-half steps.

Pre-bend:
Bend the string to the indicated pitch before picking it.

Melodic bend:
Pick the string, then bend and release the note in time with the written rhythm. (Note: parentheses in the tab notation indicate that the note, bend, or release is not picked.)

Quarter-step bend:
B.B. King typically places this microtonal bend on the tail end of a note--or bends in time with the written rhythm.

Slide:
If notes are tied, pick the string to sound the first note, then slide into the second. If notes are not tied, pick both notes. (In this example, the first and third notes are picked:)

B.B.'s bends are not always exactly a half or whole step, and often end up somewhere in between (most notably on bends involving the third, fifth, and seventh).

How to Use This Book

B.B. King's lines are drawn primarily from the major and minor pentatonic and blues scales.

Unless otherwise noted, all lines in the first section of this book are to be played as part of a standard twelve-bar blues progression in the indicated feel. (The section of this book entitled "B.B. King–Style Chord Progressions" provides a comprehensive listing of these and other progressions.) In the examples that follow, B.B. King's lines are recreated in their original form—and reflect much of their original musical intention. However, as you build a vocabulary of these lines, you will find that they can be mixed and matched in their application to your own blues guitar lines.

Here are the basic types of lines and sections that serve as the building blocks of a blues tune.

The term **chorus** refers to one cycle of the twelve-bar blues progression.

An **intro** leads into I7 lines and can sometimes be used as a I7 line or a turnaround.

A **I7 line** may be played in bars 1 through 4, 7, 8, 11, and 12.

A **IV7 line** may be played in bars 2, 5, 6, and 10.

A **V7 line** may be played in bars 9, 10, and 12.

A **turnaround** is usually played in bars 11 and 12, but may also be used as an intro.

An **ending** may also be used as an intro or turnaround.

Try playing I7 lines over the IV7 chord, or in the turnaround. Now try some V7 lines over the I7 chord. Let your ear determine whether or not each combination works. Remember: What sounds right, is right.

Try playing some of the lines that follow over the different chord progressions shown later in the book. Note the IIm-V7 and IIIm-VI7 chord movements, and experiment with all lines over these, respectively. Keep those that work for you and discard those that don't. Incorporate the useful lines into your playing as soon as possible. Stretch and vary them until they feel like your own. When you can sing or whistle them away from your guitar, they become yours for keeps.

Intros

This intro contains a call and response figure between B.B. King and the horn and rhythm sections.

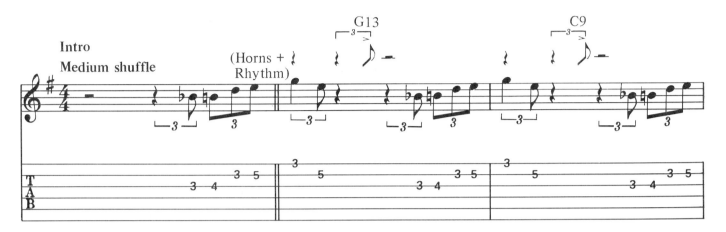

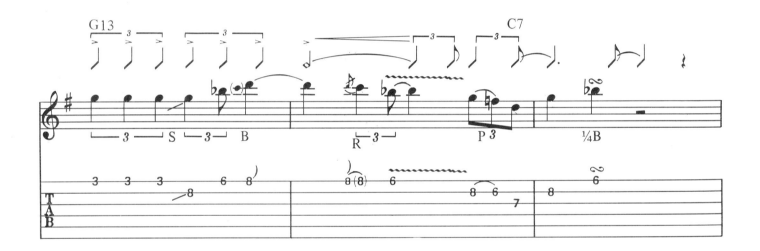

This line features a three-note pickup into a I7 chord, using a combination of triplet and sixteenth-note feels.

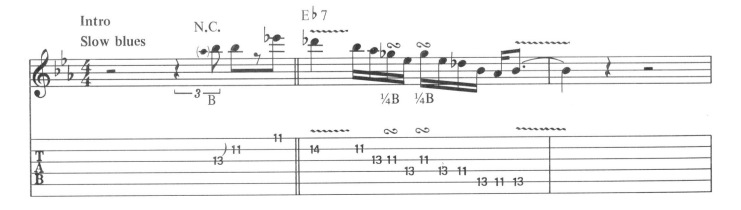

Here's a two-bar intro that can also be used as a turnaround.
Check out the use of the double stops in flatted fifths.

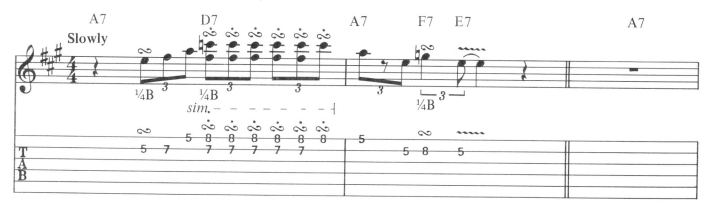

The next two examples illustrate variations on what is perhaps
B.B.'s most famous opening statement. First, here's a medium
shuffle, or slow blues, statement.

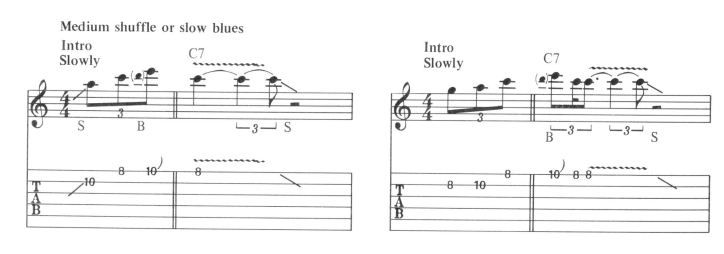

This two-bar intro with a pickup shows a jazzier chordal approach, again mixing triplet and straight sixteenth-note feels. Each seventh chord is played using a ninth fingering, allowing the bottom three notes to ring while the sixteenth-note figure is played.

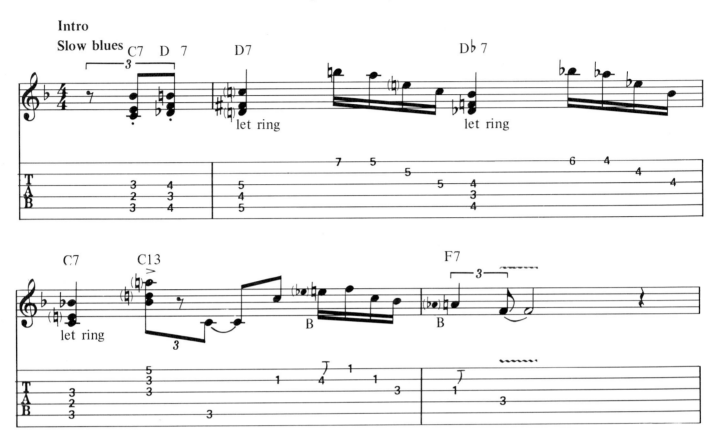

The following two lines can function either as intros or one-bar turnaround ideas (played during bar 12). Note the rhumba rhythm figure. B.B.'s note choices in these lines are clearly influenced by Charlie Christian.

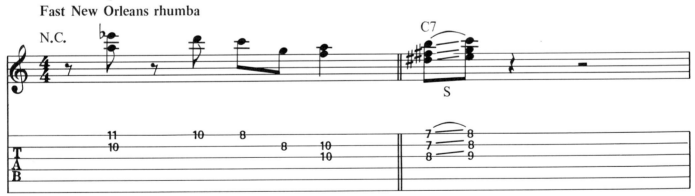

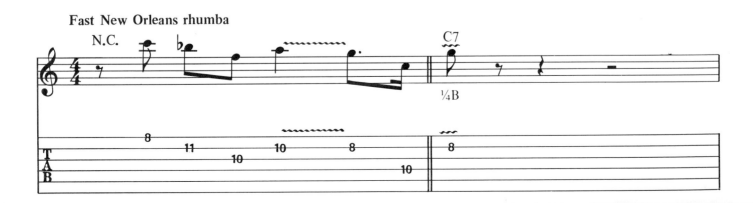

I7 Chord Lines

Some double stops in this I7 rhythm guitar figure use a hammered grace note from the minor to the major third of the I7 chord. Other double stops outline the IV chord. When combined with lower register single notes, double stops create a piano-like sound.

In bar 2 of this line, a IV7 diminished lick using double stops is superimposed over a I7 chord. Again, influences of Charlie Christian and Django Reinhardt are evident.

Here's another I7 line mixing swing and straight eighth-note groupings.

20

Here's a quick-change progression—changing to the IV chord on the second measure, then returning to the I7. This line shows B.B.'s T-Bone Walker influences.

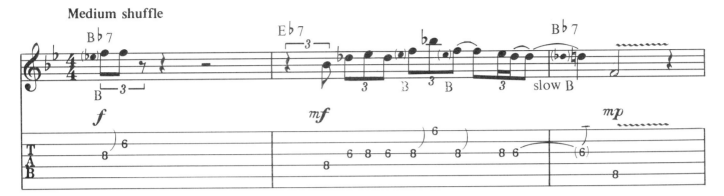

This line is played over bar 8 of a twelve-bar blues progression containing a IIIm7-VI7 chord movement, and would most likely be followed by a IIm7-V7 progression (Cm7-F7 in this key).

All eighth notes are played "straight" in this funky I7 chord lick.

Most of the accents in this I7 line are placed squarely on the beat. The upbeat accent on measure 2, beat 1, really makes it swing.

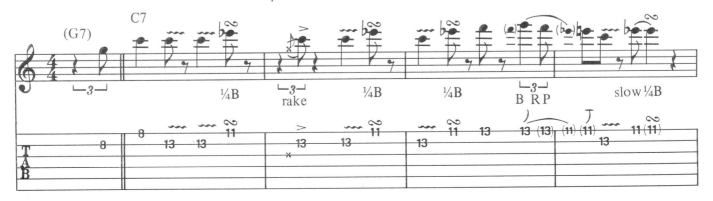

This I7 line shows a strong slide guitar influence.

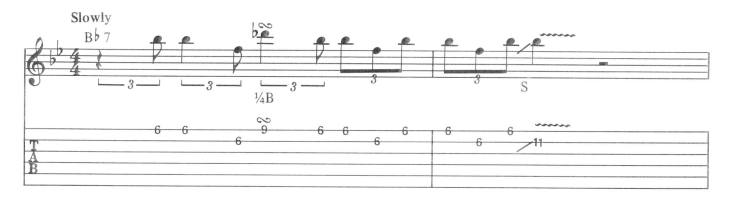

B.B. often starts a chorus with a four-bar break section. Here the rhythm section plays only the accented downbeat of each measure on the I7 chord, while he plays call and response phrases. Breaks like this often occur during vocal sections as well, with B.B.'s voice taking the role Lucille takes here.

IV7 Chord Lines

Follow this IV7 line with a I7 line.

Start this IV7-I7 movement on bar 6 of a twelve-bar blues progression (or on bar 2 if it is a quick-change pattern).

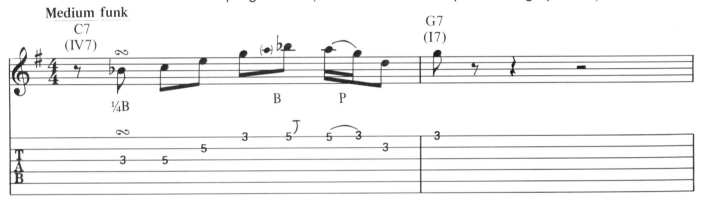

Bar 2 of this I7-IV7 line contains another of B.B.'s most famous phrases.

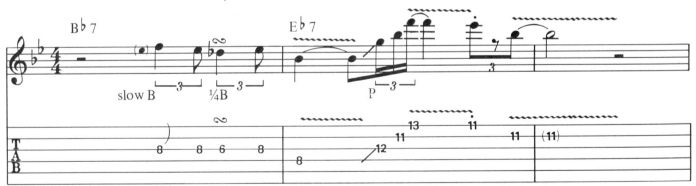

Here's another two-bar IV7 chord lick played with an eighth-note feel.

This one-bar IV7 line may be played in measures 2, 5, 6, and 10 of a twelve-bar blues.

Next is a two-bar IV7 lick, followed by a one-bar I7 resolution.

The eighth-note triplet is the main rhythm in this I7-IV7 lick, played on bars 4 and 5 of a twelve-bar blues. Try playing this one using all downstokes, then try it with alternating downstokes and upstrokes.

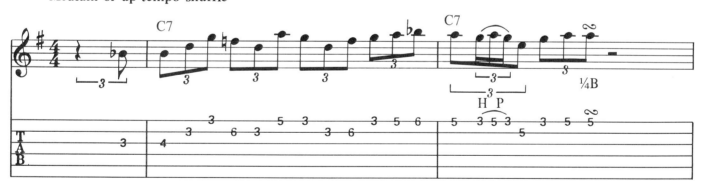

This Im-IVm line uses a rhythmic variation of a basic phrase in a call and response form.

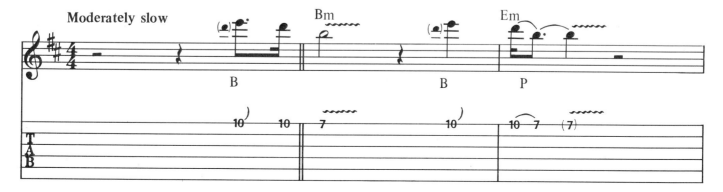

V7 Chord Lines

Here's a V7-IV7-I movement, again using straight eighth notes over a rhumba rhythm.

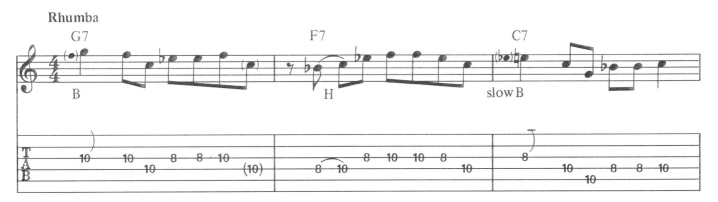

Start this V7-IV7-I7 line on bar 9 of a twelve-bar blues progression.

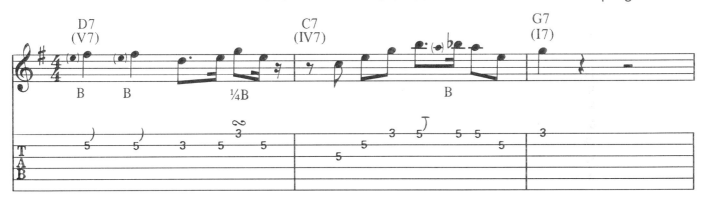

This one starts at bar 8.

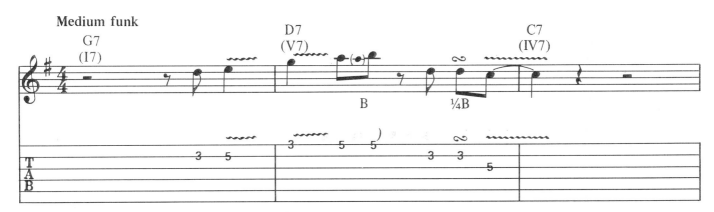

This IIm7-V7 progression works well in bars 9 and 10 of a twelve-bar blues. Try preceding it with the IIIm7-VI7 line shown previously (under the heading "I7 Chord Lines").

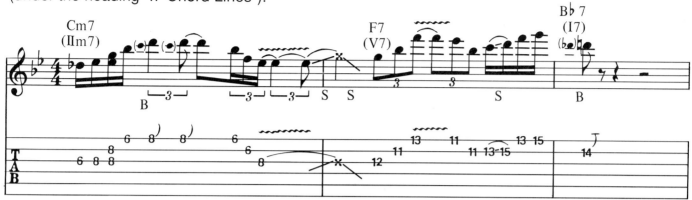

Try this V7 line on bar 9 or 12 of a twelve-bar blues progression.

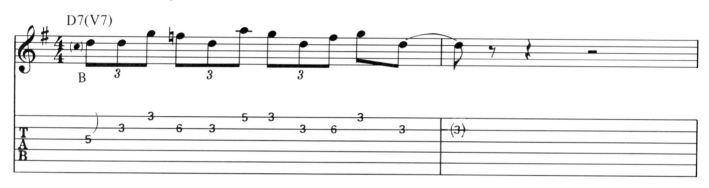

Here's a V7 lick that stretches out over two bars before moving to the I7 chord: Start it on bar 9 of a twelve-bar blues.

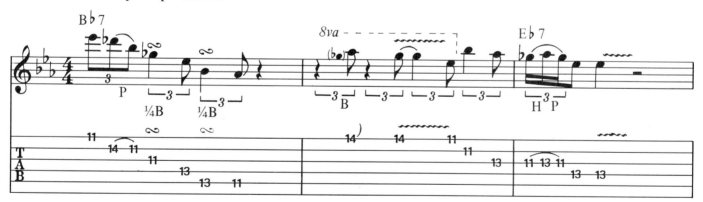

This V7-IV7 lick starts on bar 8 of a standard twelve-bar blues progression.

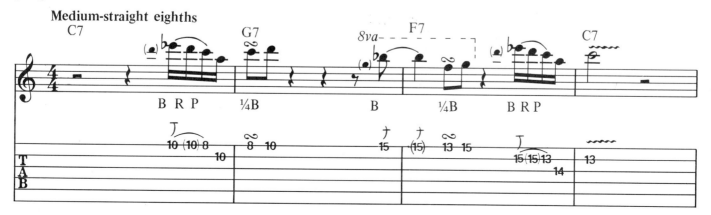

Turnarounds

The following lines are played on bars 11 and 12 of a standard twelve-bar blues progression.

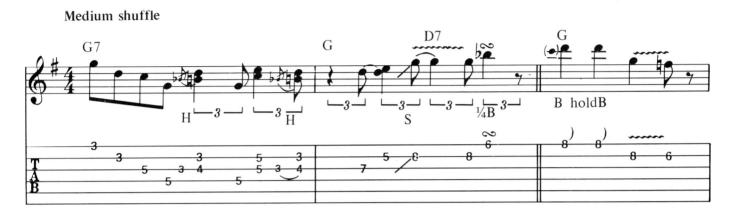

This turnaround mixes swing and straight eighth-note rhythms and contains some nice double stops.

This one-note turnaround employs a common tone between the chord changes and involves an interesting slide technique—that is, playing a note, then sliding into the same pitch on another string. Here, the influence of slide guitar technique is obvious.

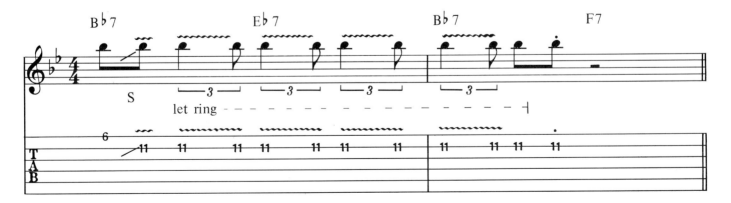

Starting with one of B.B.'s most famous phrases, this turnaround
has more complex chord movements, resulting in a new perception
of the line.

This next turnaround (I7-IV7-V7) opens with a slide-influenced lick,
followed by a typical Charlie Christian phrase, and ends with some
swinging chord punctuations. (Notice that B.B. plays B♭6 over the
F7 chord.)

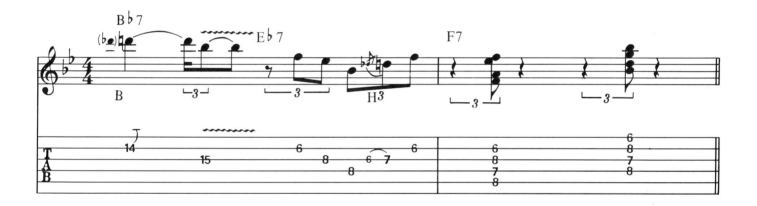

Here are four alternate turnarounds for the twelve-bar fast New
Orleans–style rhumba. These should be played on bars 11 and 12.
Note the change to a swing feel on bar 12 of the fourth turnaround
(typical of this type of progression). After a few choruses of soloing,
the rhumba figure resumes.

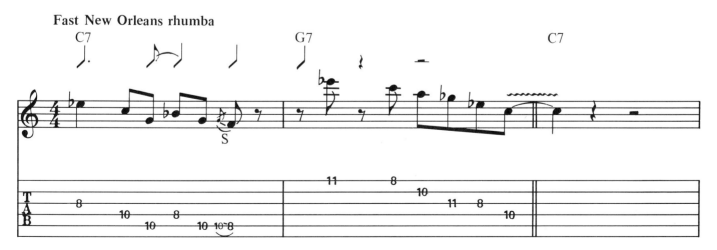

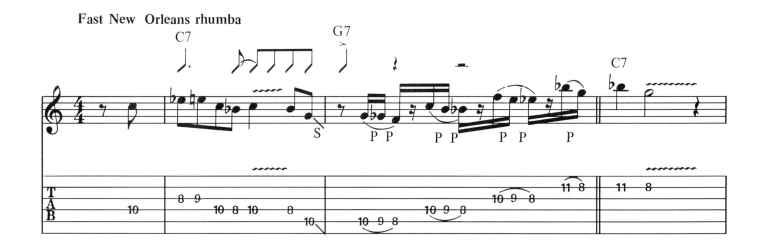

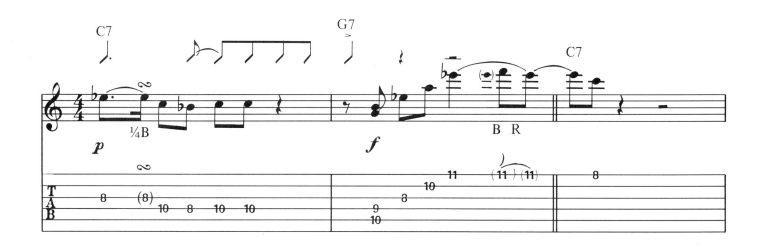

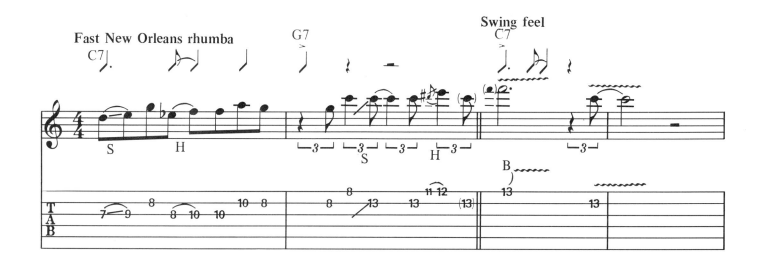

Endings

All of these endings are to be played on bars 11 and 12 of a twelve-bar blues progression: they may also be adapted to intros and turnarounds. This ending is punctuated by a swinging horn figure with stops. B.B. plays straight eighth notes.

The rhythm section plays through this straightforward ending.

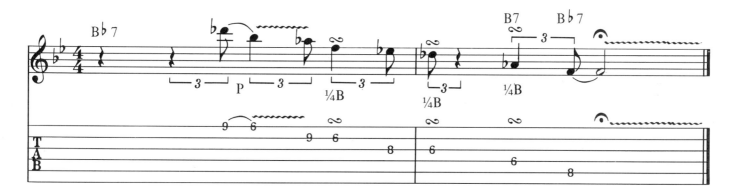

This ending features a complete stop by the rhythm and horn sections on bar 11, allowing B.B. space for a one-measure fill.

This ending features a nice chord movement (I7 IV7 #IV°V7) and a free-time guitar cadenza.

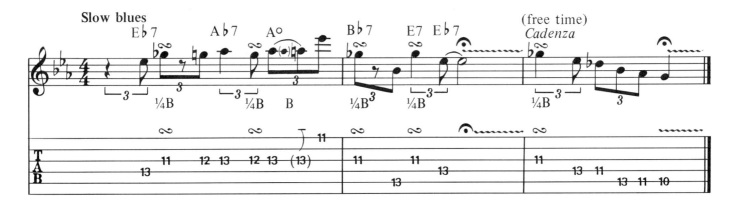

Here's one with a busier cadenza.

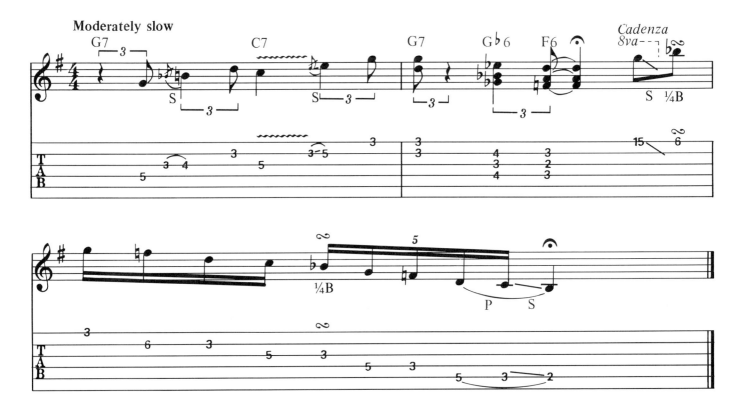

Here are some more endings for you to try.

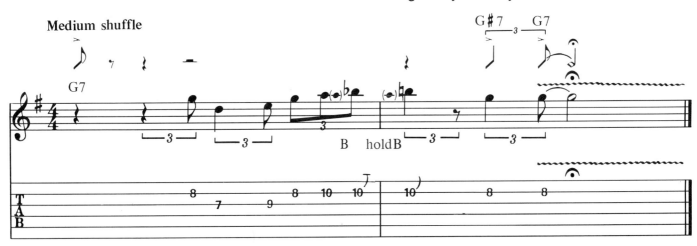

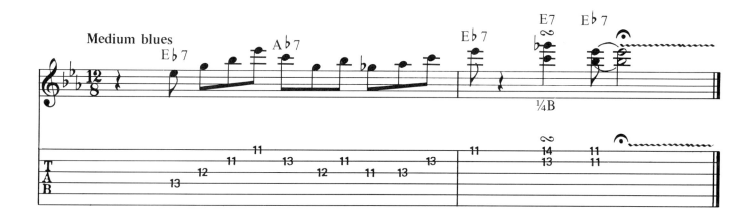

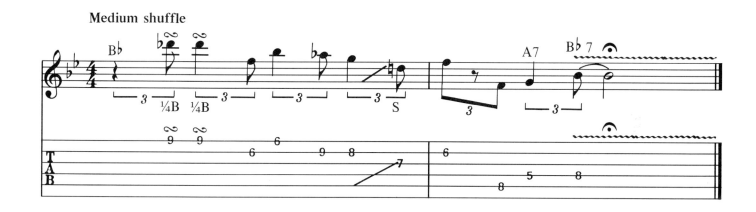

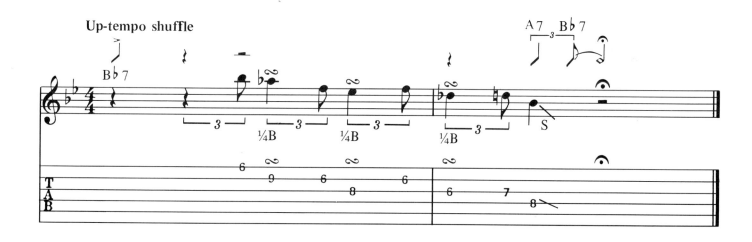

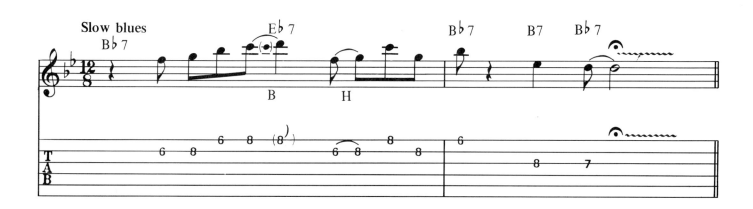

Expanding B.B. King's Lines

B.B. King's lines can be mixed and matched or, better yet, expanded on to form your own musical ideas. Combining lines and applying rhythmic displacement are two excellent ways to reinterpret your favorite phrases.

Combining Lines

This example combines two lines you have already learned.

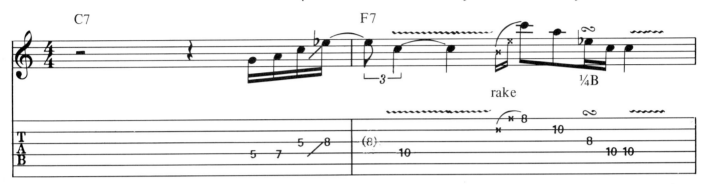

Try connecting these short phrases in a similar fashion.

Rhythmic Displacement

A line can be moved to start on any part of any beat. Displacing a line by one eighth-note is very common.

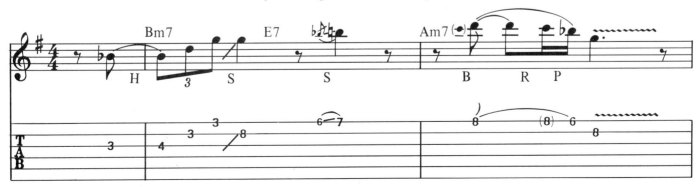

Here is the same line, starting one eighth-note later than originally written. Notice that every note in both measures is displaced by one eighth-note.

Let's take a line and displace it by one eighth-note in the opposite direction. First, here is the original line.

Now, here is the displacement by one eighth-note ahead.

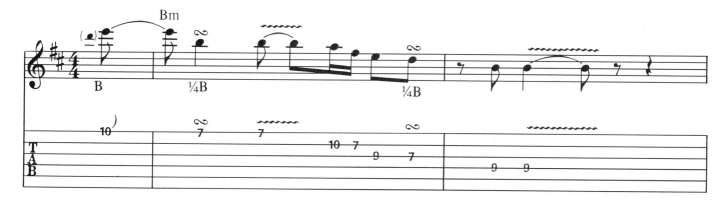

Try the lines you have just learned in different rhythmic settings, including $\frac{3}{4}$, $\frac{6}{8}$, halftime, and double-time feels. Try using swing- or shuffle-style eighths.

Swing- or shuffle-style eighth notes.

B.B. King's Solos

Woke Up This Morning

This is one of B.B. King's earliest hits. The riff is actually based on the New Orleans piano style of Professor Longhair. The rhythm section plays a vital role in the creation of this feel, with the drums playing a fast rhumba. Often the rhythm section will break into a swing rhythm on successive choruses, providing a great contrast of feels. "Woke Up This Morning" was first recorded in 1953, although this version is from 1965's *Live at the Regal*.

Woke Up This Morning
Live at the Regal
by B.B.King
Copyright © 1951 Sounds of Lucille Inc. and Powerforce Music Inc.
Copyright Renewed. International Copyright Secured. All Rights Reserved.

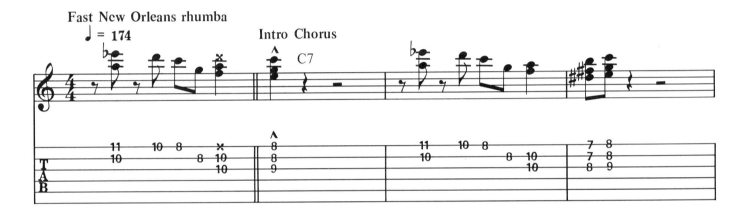

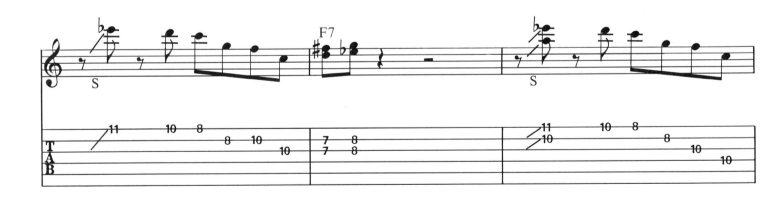

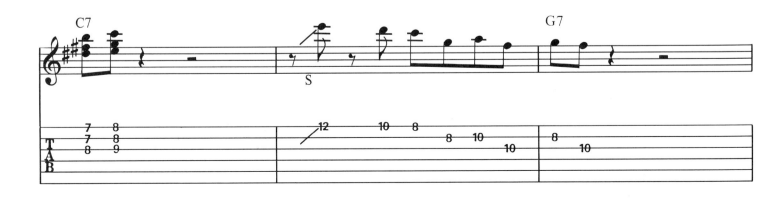

tone control to full bass position

Goin' South

Recorded much earlier than the *Live at the Regal* version of "Woke Up This Morning," this is obviously the same tune, taken from an album called *The Unexpected Instrumental B.B. King—Just Sweet Guitar* and probably retitled as a copyright matter. What matters to us is that this version kicks! Charlie Christian's influence really shines through on this chorus.

Goin' South

The Unexpected Instrumental B.B. King—Just Sweet Guitar

by B.B.King

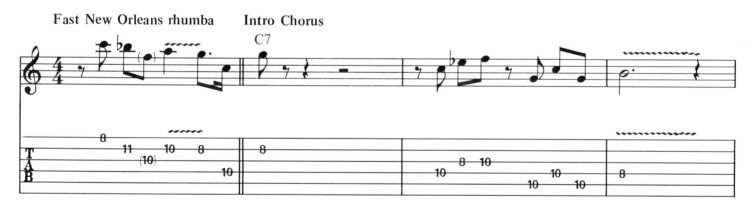

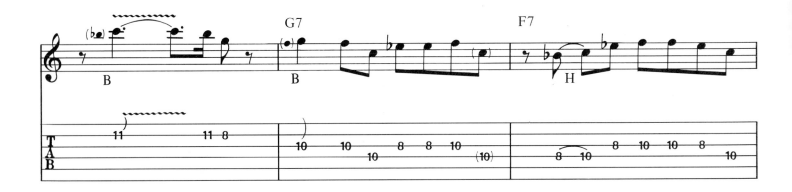

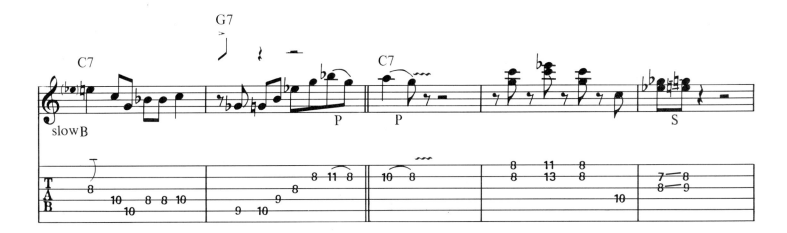

38th St. Blues

This tune features a straight eighth-note feel in the rhythm section—but that doesn't stop B.B. from swinging all over the joint! Notice the mixture of straight and swing-style eighth notes throughout this solo chorus.

38th St. Blues

The Unexpected Instrumental B.B. King—Just Sweet Guitar

by B.B.King

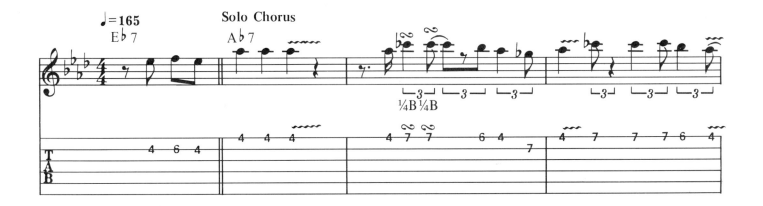

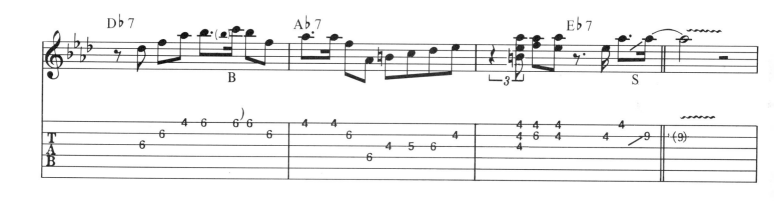

Slidin' and Glidin'

This moderately slow shuffle features some classic B.B. King licks, as well as some unusual harmonies in bars 8, 9, and 10. Check out B.B.'s note choices over this jazz-oriented progression: IIIm-VI7-IIm-V7.

Slidin' and Glidin'
The Unexpected Instrumental B.B. King—Just Sweet Guitar
by B.B.King

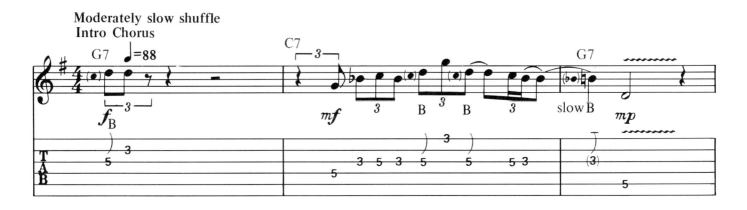

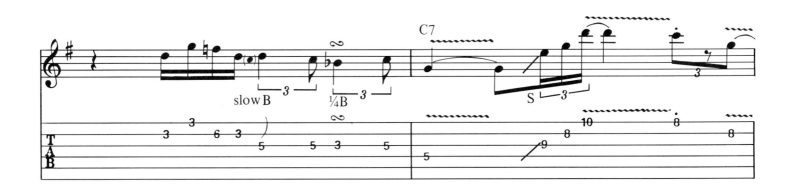

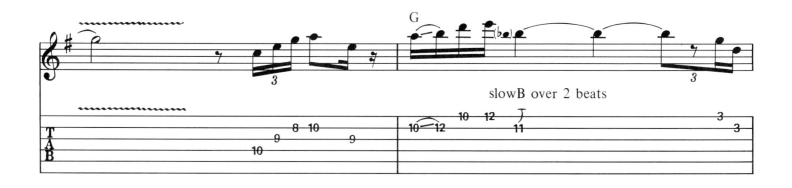

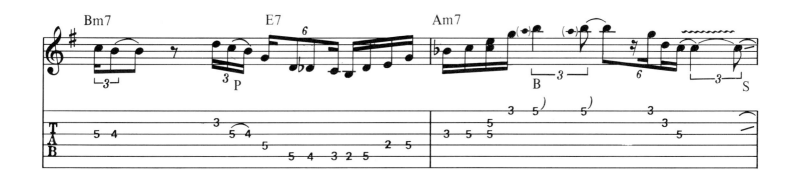

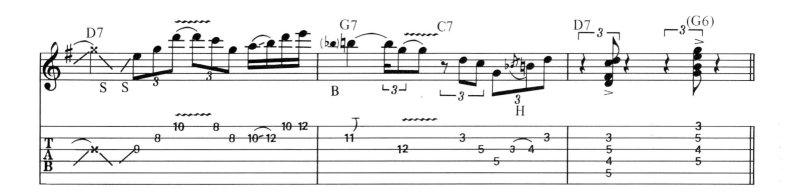

You Upsets Me, Baby

"You Upsets Me, Baby," was first released in 1959. This version was taken from a recently released CD and features a IIm-V7 change in bars 9 and 10. There are a few straight eighth notes interspersed, but this intro/chorus is played, for the most part, with a triplet feel.

You Upsets Me, Baby

studio version
Best of B.B. King, Vol. I (CD)
by J. Josea & Maxwell Davis
Copyright © 1969 Powerforce Music Inc.
International Copyright Secured. All Rights Reserved.

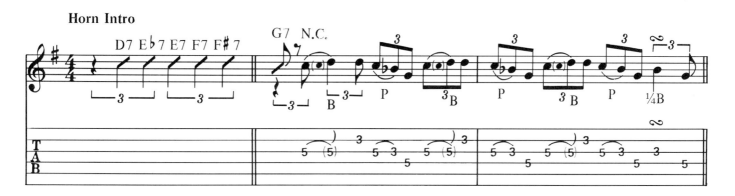

Intro Chorus

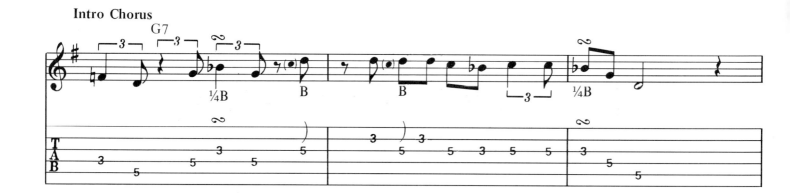

Played at a much faster tempo than the studio versions, this live arrangement of "You Upsets Me, Baby" kicks off with its signature triplet horn figure and two-bar guitar break. The intro to this classic brings to mind something that B.B. wrote in the October 1983 issue of *Guitar Player Magazine*.

> *When I was coming up, most guitarists couldn't read music. In fact, I started off the same way. You start playing by yourself, so then you cut bars—you know, play rhythm. Pretty soon, it becomes hard for anybody to play with you because you are going to play according to your feelings. You may grab the song, and when twelve bars come you might be just getting ready to go to your IV or V chord. I'd start a song, for instance, and when I was ready to make a IV change, gosh, man, maybe I played like fifteen bars before I got to that. Then sometimes may not have played two or three bars before you feel like changing. But I did learn one thing: If you have a good sense of time, a good sense of rhythm will still love you, they didn't give a darn how many bars you were making.*

B.B. and the band actually play an extra beat, but manage to pull through and finally end up together! This adds much character to the tune—and is a moment of greatness accomplished through a nearly telepathic communication with his band.

You Upsets Me, Baby

live version
Live at the Regal
by J. Josea & Maxwell Davis
Copyright © 1969 Powerforce Music Inc.
International Copyright Secured. All Rights Reserved.

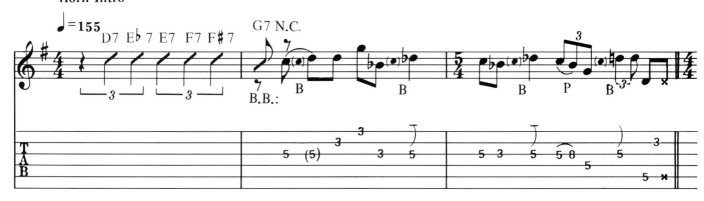

Intro Chorus

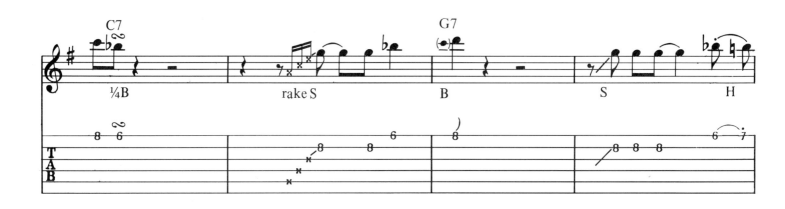

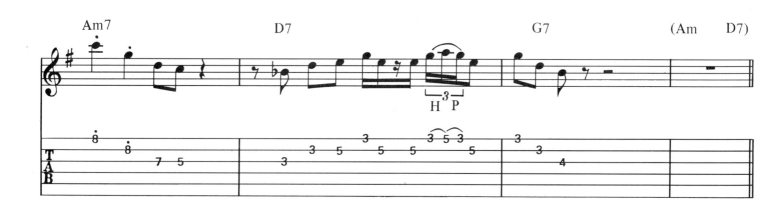

Every Day I Have the Blues

This is B.B.'s theme song, here taken from a recent CD. "Every Day I Have the Blues" opens with a jumping horn chart. B.B. answers the horn section's questions and plays some classic triplet-based phrases throughout. Have someone else play the horn figure (or prerecord it yourself) to see exactly how these phrases complement each other. The solo is also featured, including a great two-bar turnaround up front. Note that the progression switches to a standard twelve-bar form during the solo.

Every Day I Have the Blues
studio version; intro
Best of B.B. King, Vol. I (CD compilation)
by Peter Chatman
Copyright © 1969 Arc Music Corp & Fort Knox Music Inc. / Trio Music Inc.
International Copyright Secured. All Rights Reserved.

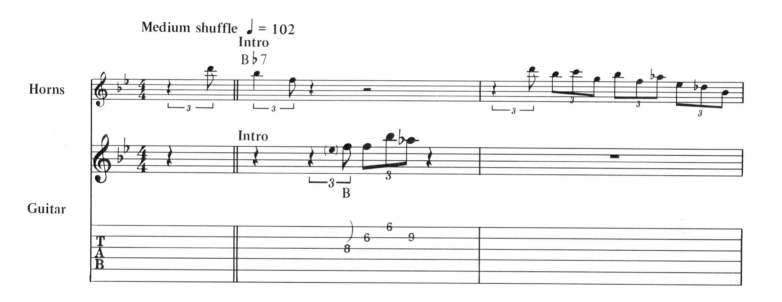

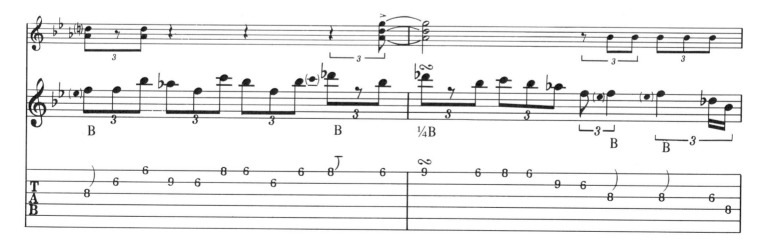

Here's the great solo, including a two-bar turnaround up front.

Every Day I Have the Blues
studio version; solo
Best of B.B. King, Vol. I
by Peter Chatman
Copyright © 1969 Arc Music Corp & Fort Knox Music Inc. / Trio Music Inc.
International Copyright Secured. All Rights Reserved.

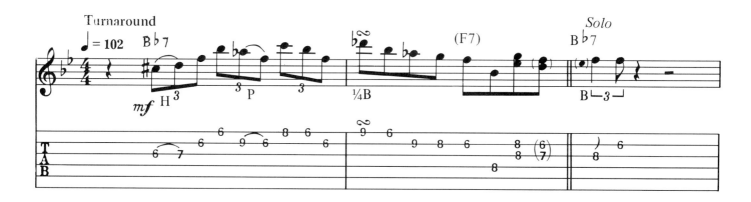

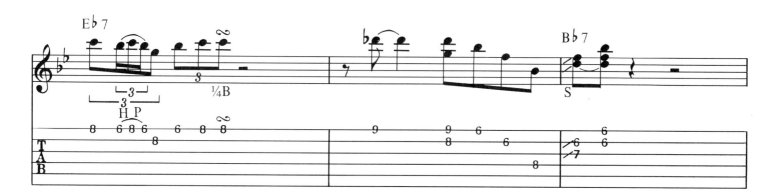

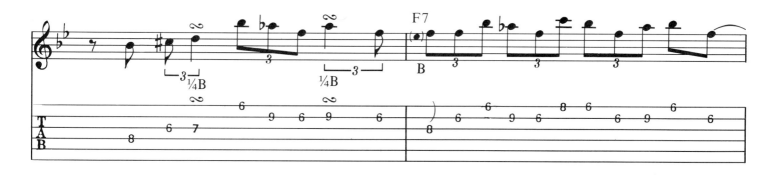

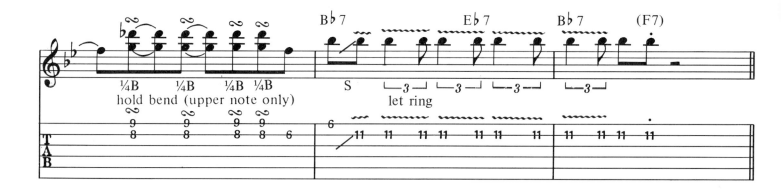

Since this is B.B.'s signature tune, it seemed appropriate to include a live intro and solo chorus from this great version. Here, the tempo is much faster and the horn chart serves as a twelve-bar intro as B.B. hits the stage and explodes into the first chorus. There are new changes in the progression as well, including a new turnaround.

Every Day I Have the Blues

live version; intro/chorus
Live at the Regal
by Peter Chatman

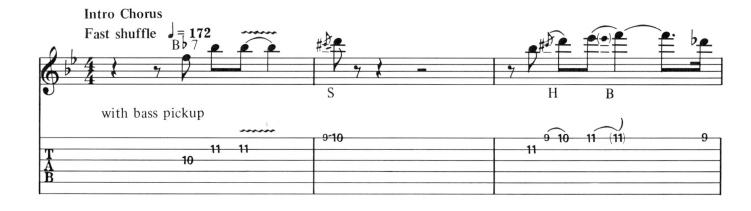

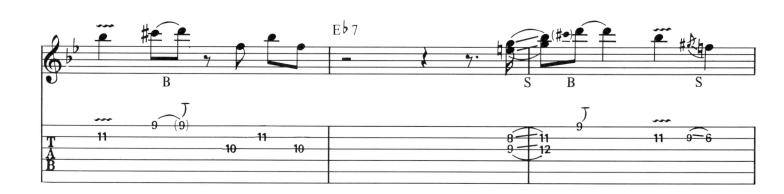

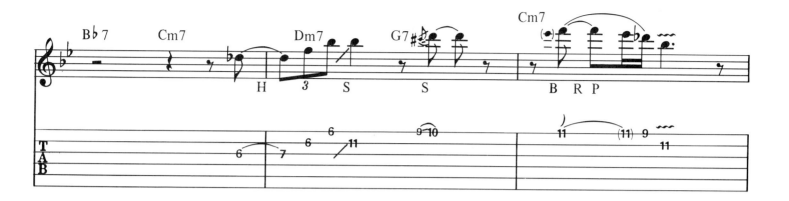

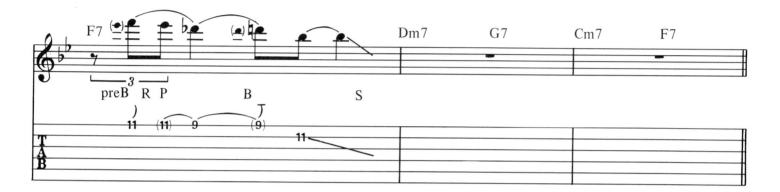

This next chorus is B.B.'s second solo chorus. After playing through the first, using the bass (neck position) pickup with most of the treble rolled off, he switches pickups and cranks it back on, propelling his solo to the next level of excitement. The influence of Charlie Christian is clear in bars 8 and 9.

Every Day I Have the Blues
live version; fourth chorus
Live at the Regal
by Peter Chatman

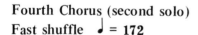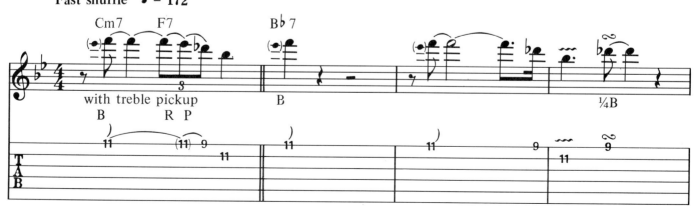

48

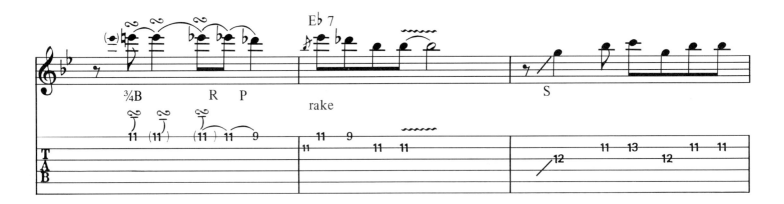

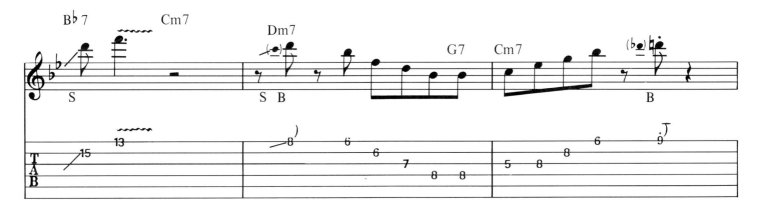

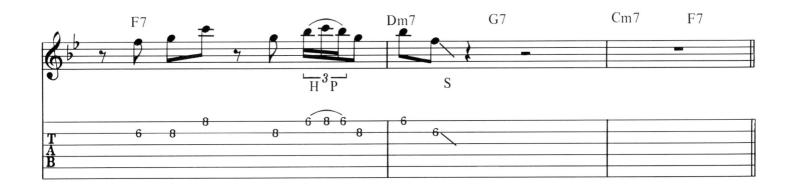

Sweet Little Angel

Notating B.B.'s phrasing in slower tempos is a bit tricky. In "Sweet Little Angel," he plays off of the $\frac{12}{8}$ pulse. This rhythm is actually generated by an extremely slow $\frac{4}{4}$ pulse. As a result, each beat (or dotted quarter note) may be thought of as a mini-measure of $\frac{3}{4}$ time. For instance, this one measure of $\frac{12}{8}$.

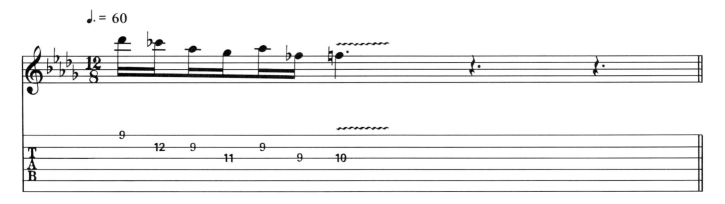

may be thought of as four measures of fast $\frac{3}{4}$.

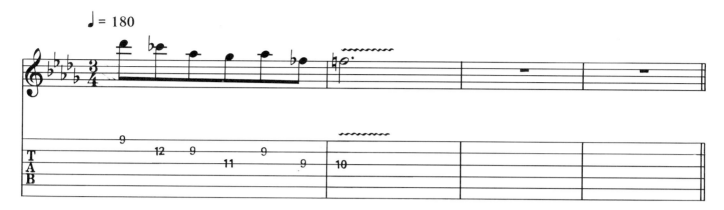

Here's another example.

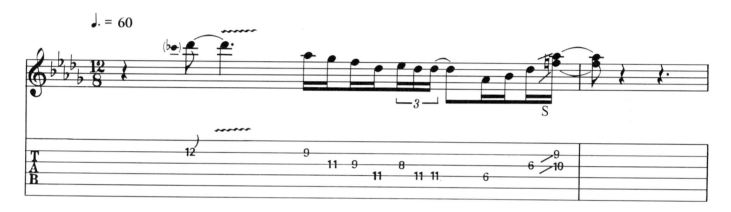

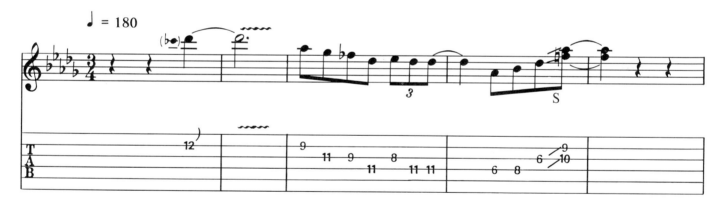

B.B. mixes straight sixteenth-note rhythms with those derived from the triplet feel in this classic lick. Although they are notated as an eighth-note quadruplet in $\frac{12}{8}$, these are felt the same way that normal sixteenth notes would be over a slow $\frac{4}{4}$ pulse.

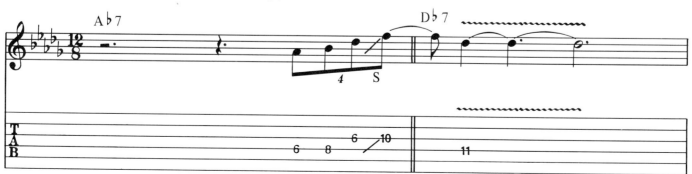

Notice the slide into the major third of the I7 chord. By flatting the third, you can create a D♭m7 line. This works well as a IV7 line. Once understood, these lines can be altered and extended to form many similar lines.

Sweet Little Angel
live version
Live at the Regal
by Riely B. King & J. Taub
Copyright © 1969 Powerforce Music Inc. & Sounds of Lucille Inc.
International Copyright Secured. All Rights Reserved.

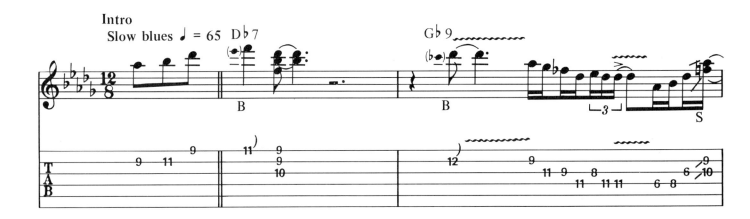

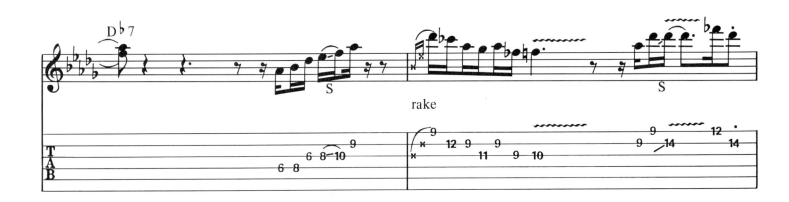

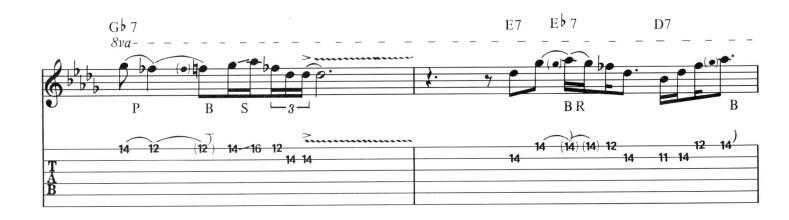

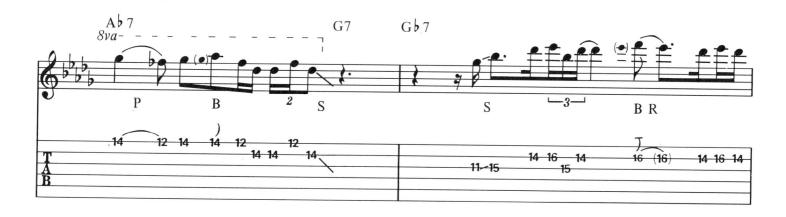

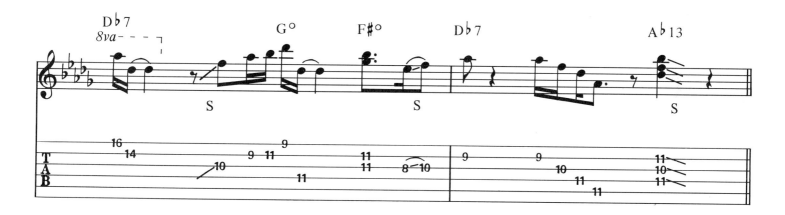

Why I Sing the Blues

This 1969 version of B.B.'s classic was played with a straight eighth-note feel at a medium tempo with a funky rhythm-section groove. B.B. plays it straight in this chorus, with only one swing triplet figure throughout.

Why I Sing the Blues
Live and Well

by B.B. King & Dave Clark
Copyright © 1969 Sounds of Lucille Inc.and Duchess Music Inc.
International Copyright Secured. All Rights Reserved.

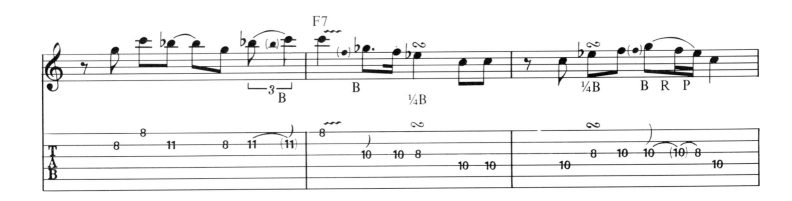

The Thrill Is Gone

These next choruses from B.B.'s biggest hit will provide enough ideas to guide you through any minor blues. Note the amount of restraint B.B. applies in playing these solos. Listen to the recording and check out how quietly they are played. When an occasional phrase is accented with an increase in volume, it really speaks out. The intro is played with only the rhythm section as accompaniment, while the rest of the tune features a string orchestra.

The Thrill Is Gone
intro
Completely Well
by R. Hawkins & R. Darnell

Intro
Moderately slow

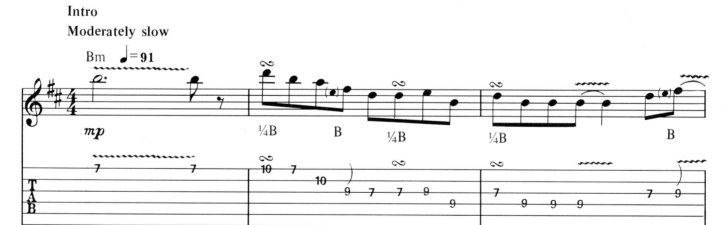

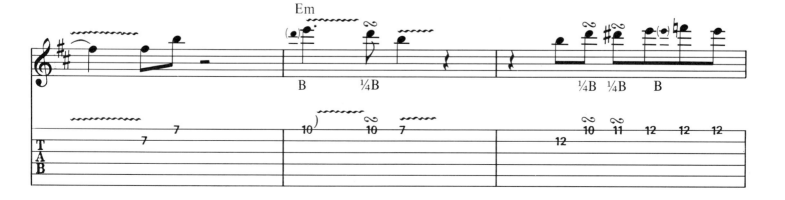

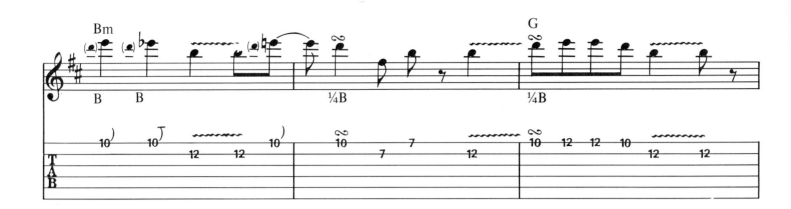

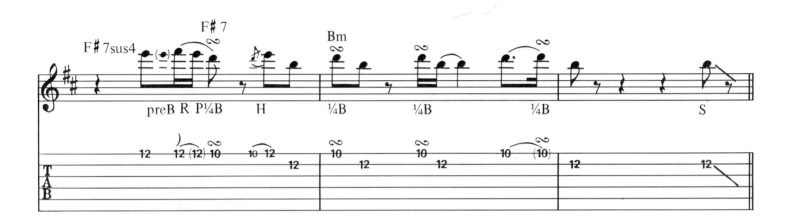

B.B.'s first solo and the string accompaniment are transcribed here. It's hard to say whether B.B. recorded his solos before or after the strings were added, but the result sure is fine.

The Thrill Is Gone

solo
Completely Well

by R. Hawkins & R. Darnell
Copyright © 1951 Sounds of Lucille Inc. and Powerforce Music Inc.
Copyright Renewed. International Copyright Secured. All Rights Reserved.

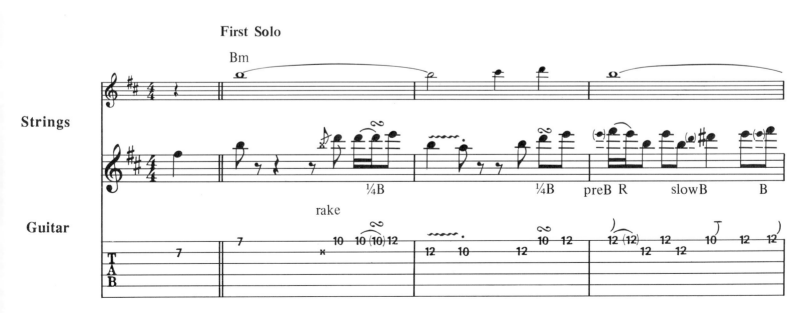

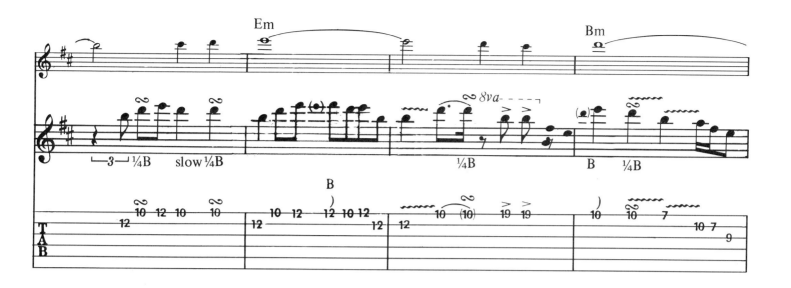

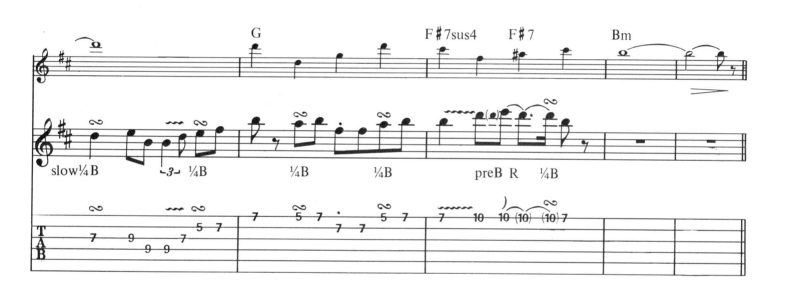

B.B. King—Style Chord Voicings

B.B. is not known for his rhythm playing, but has been known to use voicings like those shown below throughout the years. Try these out for yourself.

Dominant and Altered Dominant Sounds

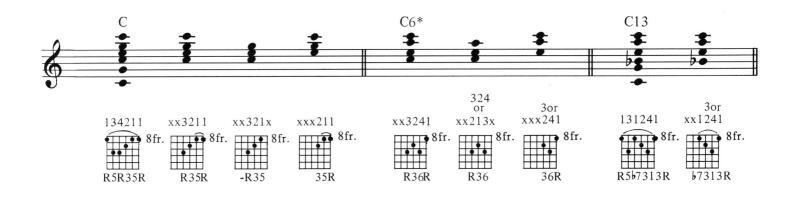

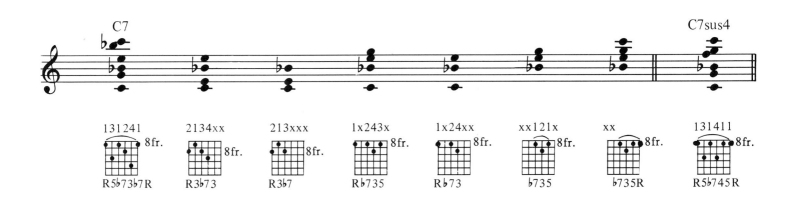

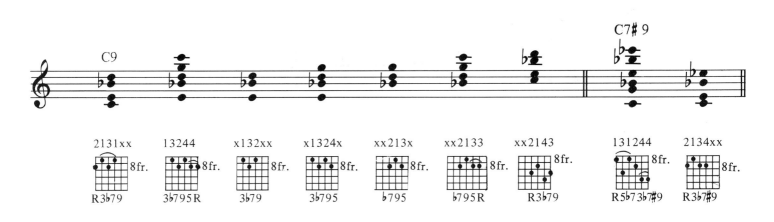

* C6 does not contain a ♭7, however it is a common substitute for C7.

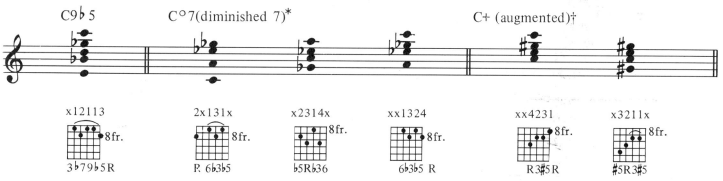

C9♭5   C°7(diminished 7)*   C+ (augmented)†

x12113   2x131x   x2314x   xx1324   xx4231   x3211x

8fr. (for each diagram)

3♭79♭5R   R 6♭3♭5   ♭5R♭36   6♭3♭5 R   R3♯5R   ♯5R3♯5

All of these voicings are derived from the first-position E major chord shape, transposed to C.

*Note that a diminished seventh chord becomes inverted when moved a minor third (one and one-half steps) in either direction. This means that any note in the chord can function as the root—so only three different diminished chords are possible. This chord functions as a C♯7♭9.

† An augmented chord is built of major thirds and functions as C7♯5 without the seventh. Try it as the V7 chord in a turnaround.

This table includes all voicings derived from the first-position A major chord shape, transposed to C (except where noted).

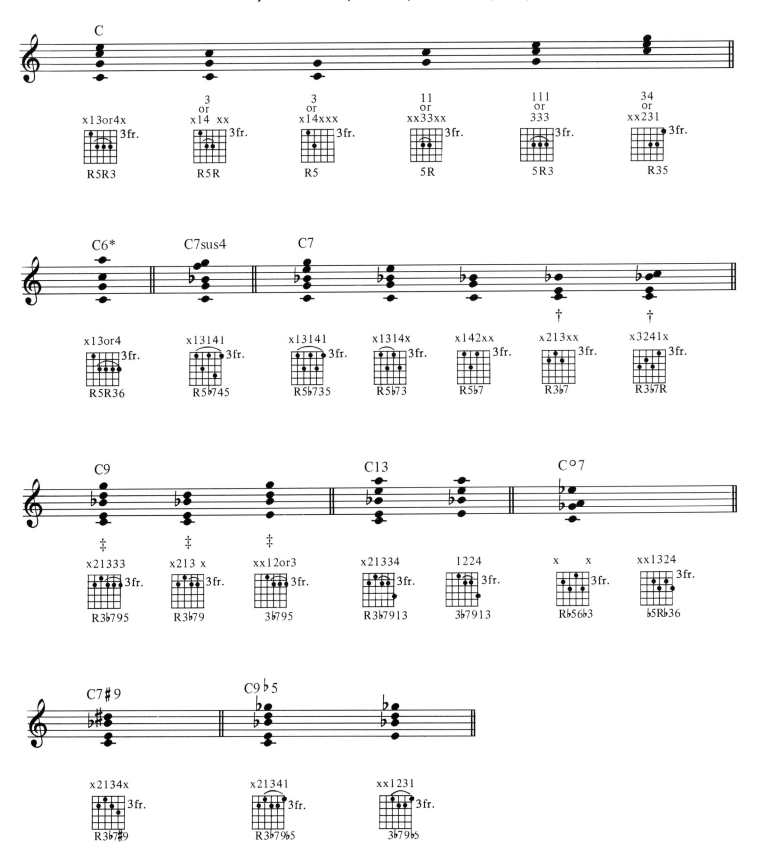

*Again, C6 contains no ♭7, but is commonly used in place of C7. Try this voicing as an ending chord.

†Derived from the first-position C major chord shape.

‡ Derived from both A and C major chord shapes.

Major Seventh Voicings

Derived from the first-position E major chord shape, transposed to C.

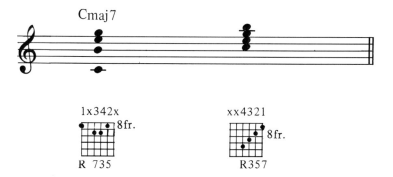

Derived from the first-position A major chord shape, transposed to C.

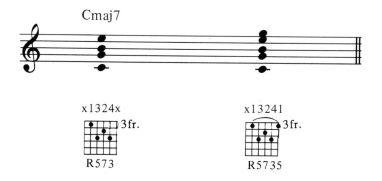

Derived from the first-position C major chord shape.

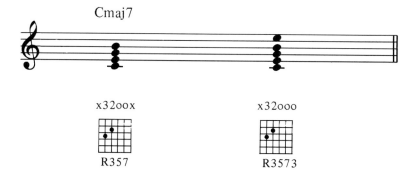

60

Minor Voicings

Derived from the first-position E minor chord shape, transposed to C.

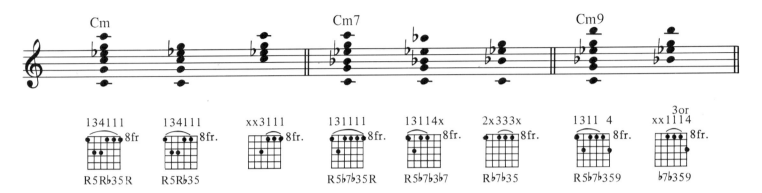

Derived from the first-position A minor chord shape, transposed to C.

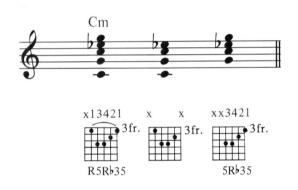

Derived from the first-position C minor chord shape.

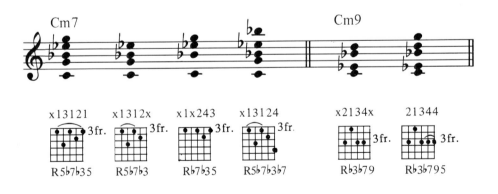

B.B. King—Style Chord Progressions

Using a figured bass system, many different chord progressions can be illustrated without being associated with a particular key.

The notes of the chromatic scale are indicated using the following roman numerals and accidentals: I, ♭II, II, ♭III, III, IV, ♯IV (♭V), V, ♯V (♭VI), VI, ♭VII and VII. Each numeral corresponds to a half-step of the chromatic scale in a given key. For example, in the key of C, notes correspond to their figured bass numerals, as follows:

C	D♭	D	E♭	E	F	F♯	(G♭)	G	G♯	(A♭)	A	B♭	B
I	♭II	II	♭III	III	IV	♯IV	(♭V)	V	♯V	(♭VI)	VI	♭VII	VII

If you are not already familiar with figured bass notation, make a chart similar to the one above for each key. These charts will help you to determine which root tone corresponds to a given roman numeral—and can be very handy during practice. For instance, the chord symbol I7 indicates that you build a dominant seventh chord on the first degree of the scale. IV9 indicates that you play a dominant ninth based on the fourth degree, and so on. If nothing appears after the numeral, just play a major chord. When two roman numerals are separated by a slash (I/V), play the top numeral as a chord, with the bass note indicated by the bottom numeral.

Here are some different chords, illustrated in the key of C.

I = C	I7 = C7	Im = Cm	I△7 = C Major7
I+ = C augmented	I9 = C9	Im7 = Cm7	Isus4 = Csus4
I°7 = C diminished 7	I7♯9 = C7♯9	I6 = C6	I/V = C/G
			I/♭VII =C/B♭
			I/III = C/E

Now the basic twelve-bar blues progression.

Here's a variation of that progression using a quick change to the IV7 chord in bar 2, and a slightly different turnaround. Both progressions may be played in different tempos, including slow, medium, and uptempo shuffles, straight eighth-note feels, $\frac{12}{8}$ time, and various funk grooves.

Here's a twelve-bar intro and a sixteen-bar verse (with breaks) that switches back to the intro for solos.

Here is an eight-bar progression with a bridge.

Try these other typical progressions.

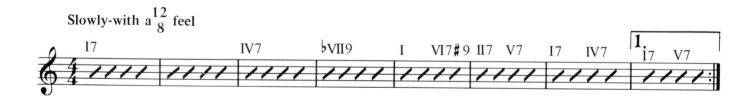

64

Medium shuffle

Slow $\frac{12}{8}$ feel

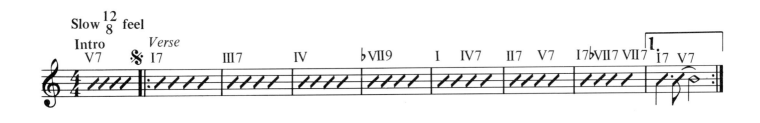

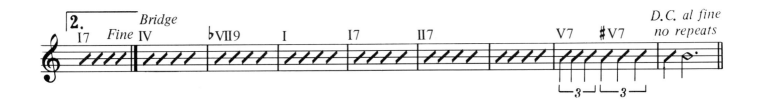

Watch out for the key changes in this next one. (This progression is also shown written out in the key of C later on.)

* Key change to the relative major key—so ♭III = I of the new key.

† Key change back to relative minor—thus III7 becomes V7 of the relative minor key (note that the vamp stays in the relative major key).

Here are some more useful blues progressions.

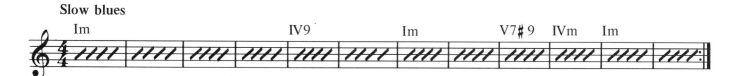

66

The complete form of this next one is Intro AABAA. The A section may be repeated for solos or as an outro.

Here's one that alternates between New Orleans rhumba and swing feels.

New Orleans rhumba

Swing

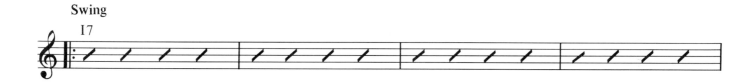

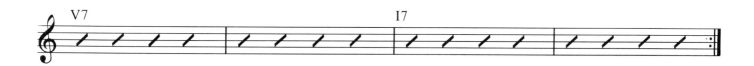

By experimenting with different rhythms and feels, endless variations are possible. If no specific rhythm figure is indicated, a part is shown using four quarter-note slashes (////) per bar. For variation, you might play an eighth-note triplet figure for each quarter note. In other words, during the four-beat bar (////), play the following:

Here is an example of how the basic twelve-bar blues progression may be transposed into various keys.

Key of C

Key of G

Key of B♭

As a further example, here is one of the more complex progressions from above transposed to the key of C.

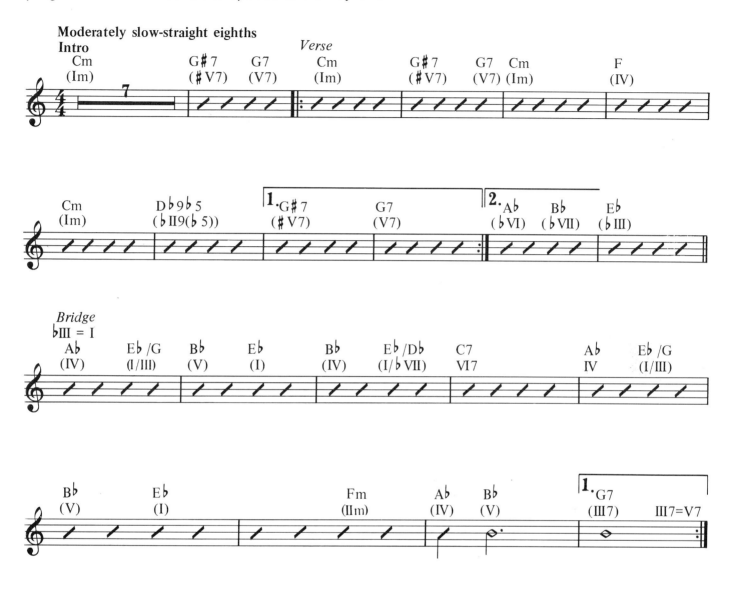

Once you feel comfortable with these progressions, try to mix and match them to create your own blues tunes. Good luck, and keep practicing.

Discography

Titles followed by an asterisk are available in CD.

Across the Tracks (Ace CHD-230)
Ambassador of the Blues (Crown Gem-001)
Anthology of the Blues (Kent 9011)
B.B. King in London (ABC 730)
Back in the Alley (MCA D-878)
Best of B.B. King (MCA 27-074)*
Best of B.B. King, Vol. I (Ace CH 198)
Best of B.B. King, Vol. II (Ace CH 199)*
Better than Ever (Kent 561)
Blues Is King (Bluesway 6001)
Blues 'n' Jazz (MCA 27119)
Blues 'n' Jazz/The Electric Book (MCA D-5881) (double CD) *
Blues on Top of Blues (Bluesway 6011)
Boss of the Blues (Kent 529)
Completely Well (MCA 27009)*
Confessin' the Blues (ABC 528)
Doin' My Thing, Lord (Kent 563)
Electric B.B. King (MCA D813)
Electric B.B. King—His Best (MCA 27007)
From the Beginning (Kent 533)
Great Moments w/B.B. King (MCA2-4124)*
Greatest Hits of B.B. King (Kent 552)
Guess Who? (ABC 759)
Guitar Player (MCA 2-8012)
His Best—The Electric B.B. King (Bluesway 6022)
Incredible Soul of B.B. King (Kent 539)
Indianola Mississippi Seeds (ABC 713-B)
The Jungle (Kent 521)
King of the Blues Guitar (Ace CH-152)
Kingsize (AB 977)
L.A. Midnight (ABC 734)
Let Me Love You (Kent 513)
Live and Well (MCA 27008)*
Live at the Regal (MCA 27006)*
Live at the Regal/Live at Cook County Jail (MCA D-5877) (double CD)*
Live, B.B. King on Stage (Kent 515)
Live in Cook County Jail (MCA 27005)*
Live, "Now Appearing" at Ole Mississippi (MCA 2-8016)
Love Me Tender (MCA 886)
Lucille (Bluesway 6016)
Lucille Talks Back (ABC)
Memphis Masters (Ace CH-50)
Midnight Believer (MCA 27011)
Mr. Blues (ABC 456)
My Kind of Blues (Crown 5188)
One-Nighter Blues (Ace CHD201)
Original "Sweet 16" (Kent 568)
Pure Soul (Kent 517)

Rhythm and Blues Christmas (UA LW-654)
Rock and Roll Festival, Vol. I (Kent 544)
Rock Me Baby (Kent 512) (Ace CH 119)
Six Silver Strings (MCA 5616)*
Sixteen Original Big Hits (Stax 4508)
Spotlight on Lucille (Ace CDCH-187)* (CD only)
Take It Home (MCA 31-51)
There Must Be a Better Word (MCA 27034)
To Know You (ABC X794)
Turn On to B.B. King (Kent 548)
Twenty Super R&B Hits (Kent 530)
Underground Blues (Kent 535)
The Unexpected Instrumental B.B. King—Just Sweet Guitar (Kent KLC 2002)

B.B. also recorded approximately ten untitled Crown releases (all out of print) in the mid-fifties.

Recordings With Other Artists

Into the Night (music from soundtrack) (MCA 27108)
Together Again (MCA 27012)
With Bobby Blue Bland: Together for the First Time
(MCA 7-50190)*